What do we think about

Adoption?

Jillian Powell

WAYLAND

Titles in the series

What do we think about ...

Adoption • Alcohol • Bullying
Death • Disability • Drugs
Family Break-Up • Our Environment

All Wayland books encourage children to read and help them improve their literacy.

✓ The contents page, page numbers, headings and index help locate specific pieces of information.

✓ The glossary reinforces alphabetic knowledge and extends vocabulary.

✓ The further information section suggests other books dealing with the same subject.

✓ Find out more about how this book is specifically relevant to the National Literacy Strategy on page 31.

Editor: Elizabeth Gogerly
Consultant: John Bennett, a Health Education Coordinator
Cover designer: Jan Sterling
Designer: Jean Wheeler
Photo researcher/stylist: Gina Brown
Production controller: Carol Titchener

First published in 1999 by Wayland Publishers Limited,
61 Western Road, Hove, East Sussex BN3 1JD

Find Wayland on the Internet at http://www.wayland.co.uk

British Library Cataloguing in Publication Data
British Library Cataloguing in Publication Data

Powell, Jillian
What do we think about adoption?
1. Adoption – Juvenile literature
I. Title II. Adoption
362. 7' 34

ISBN 07502 2492 4

Printed and bound by Eurografica S.p.A in Marano, Italy

Picture acknowledgements

Cover (main) Martyn F. Chillmaid (background) Dennis Day

Eye Ubiquitous 6; Sally Greenhill 8; Topham 13; Tony Stone Image 24.
All other photography by Family Life Pictures/ Angela Hampton.

Contents

What is adoption?

Every one of us has birth parents,
a birth mum and a birth dad.

Sometimes, our birth parents can't look after us when we are babies or as we grow up.

If this happens, we may be adopted by new parents. If you are adopted, you have adoptive parents as well as your birth parents.

Why are some people adopted?

Sometimes our birth parents can't look after us because they are ill or they have died.

Some children are adopted from other countries because they have lost their birth families because of war.

Other children are adopted because their birth parents are too young to look after them. Sometimes the mother is all by herself and can't cope alone.

Who is adopted?

Millions of people around the world are adopted. Children can be adopted when they're babies or when they're older.

You may not know just by looking at a person whether he or she is adopted or not.

You may have a brother, a sister or a friend who is adopted, or perhaps you were adopted yourself.

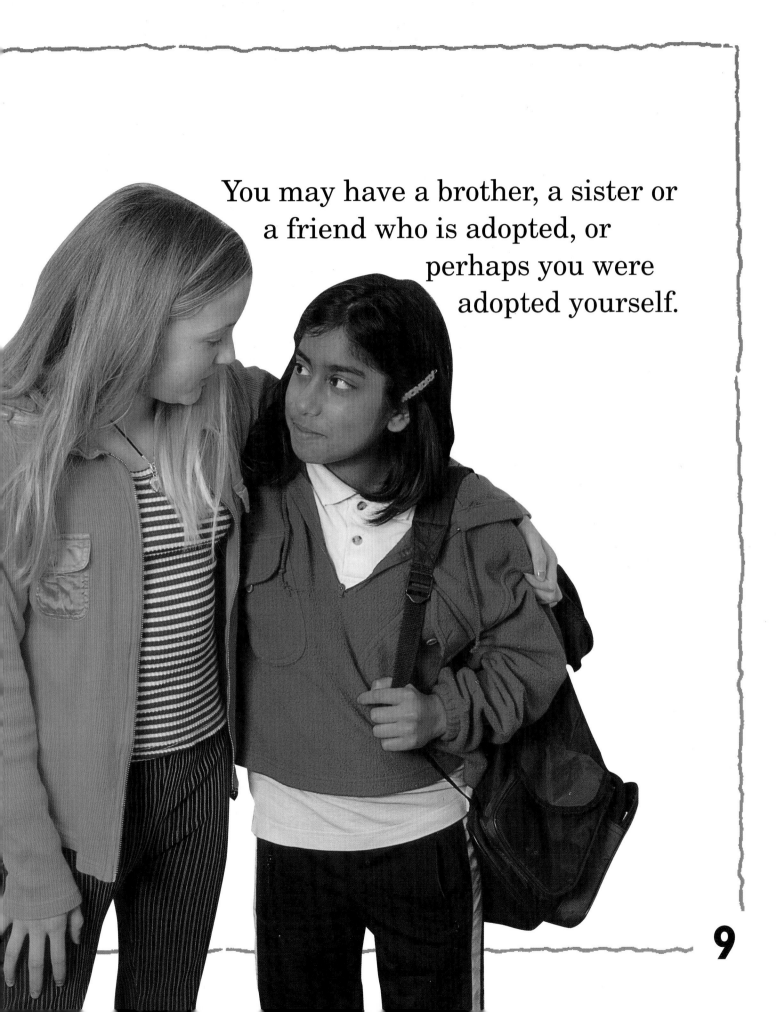

What does being adopted mean?

When you are adopted, you become part of a new family. Your adoptive parents will love you and take care of you.

Simon was adopted when he was a baby. His adoptive parents, Susan and Adam, love him very much.

Simon was adopted twelve years ago. He knows that Susan and Adam really wanted him because they adopted him.

Simon knows that they will always love him and they will always be his adoptive parents. Adoption is for ever.

Who are adoptive parents?

All kinds of people become adoptive parents, but they all want a child very much.

They may not be able to have babies of their own, or they may already have children but want a bigger family.

Some children are adopted by their step-parent, or by relatives such as grandparents or an aunt and uncle.

Isabel was adopted by her uncle Max because her own parents had died.

What happens when someone is adopted?

When someone wants to adopt a child they contact an adoption agency. A social worker from the agency then visits them at their home.

The social worker asks them lots of questions. They then try to find a child who would be happy with this family.

Kate and Pete want to adopt a child because they can't have any babies of their own.

They are lucky. The adoption agency have found a child for them to adopt. Kate and Pete are now looking forward to welcoming her into their home.

What is a foster family?

Foster carers look after children when their birth parents can't look after them properly. The children still belong to their birth parents but they are cared for by a foster family for a while.

Later they may go back to their birth parents, or they may be adopted.

When Gita's mother was ill she was fostered by
Ben and Milly. They looked after Gita for a few
months until her mother was well again.

Who are foster carers?

Foster carers can be a single person or a couple. They may have no children of their own or they may have a big family.

Sometimes they have fostered lots of children at different times. All kinds of people become foster carers, but they all love and care for children.

What about your birth parents?

Some people are adopted when they are very
young so they can't remember their birth
parents. Jane sometimes gets upset and would
like to know more about her birth parents.

She finds talking about this with her adoptive parents helps. They help her to understand why she had been adopted. They also tell her how much they love her.

Can you meet your birth parents?

If you are adopted, you may know quite a lot about your birth parents already. You might have photographs and remember times when you were together.

Jack still writes to his birth father. His father sends Jack gifts, such as this book. They also meet each year on Jack's birthday.

Some children don't meet their birth parents until they are older. Robbie was eighteen when he decided to meet his birth mother. Now they meet every week.

Robbie still thinks of his adoptive mother as his real mum though.

What about your new family?

When you are adopted, you become part of a family. You may not look like your adoptive parents but adoptive children often begin to be like their family in other ways.

When you are adopted you might have other brothers or sisters by adoption. All of you will be part of the same family and you will grow up together as a family.

Does being adopted make you different?

When you are adopted, you will become part of a whole new family. Your new life might be very different but the most important thing is that you are loved.

Your new parents chose you. They will love you just as much as if you were their birth child.

Notes for parents and teachers

Read this book with children one to one or in groups. Ask them if they can explain what adoption means. Ask them to think of as many reasons as they can why someone might be adopted.

Encourage each child to make a 'life story' book. This can be a scrap book or album and could include photographs, drawings, cards, train tickets, and written memories and descriptions.

Each child could also write their own birth story such as where they were born, who their parents are and what they know about them.

Adopted children may be sensitive on the issue of physical resemblance. Talk to the children about other ways in which we may take after our parents, such as the way we say or do things, the things we like doing, and the things that make us laugh. Point out that adoptive children can become so much like their adoptive parents that people often have no idea that they are adopted.

Talk about other kinds of adoption. The class or school could adopt an animal at a local nature park or zoo, or a local building in need of funding. This could provide the stimulus for drawing and writing from observation, and for projects to raise funds.

Explain how some people decide to try to trace their birth parents with the help of adoption agencies. Talk about some of the issues this raises, such as how children and adoptive parents may feel, and the fact that some birth parents may wish to be contacted, and others may not.

Ask the children if they understand what fostering means. Ask them to think of some of the reasons why children may need to be fostered. Explain the difference between long-stay and short-stay fostering. Talk about the care provided by foster and children's homes.

Glossary

adoption agency A place where people go when they want to adopt a child.

adoptive parents Parents who have adopted a child.

birth parents The parents who gave birth to you.

foster carers Parents who look after a child for a while when their birth parents are not able to.

social worker Someone who helps families and elderly people, especially if they are poor or in any kind of trouble.

Further information

Books to read

If you are adopted British Agencies for Adoption and Fostering
  Advice Notes (1997)
My Book About Me National Foster Care Association (1992)
What's happening? Adoption by Karen Bryant-Mole
  (Wayland, 1992)

Organizations which help people with adoption

British Agencies for
Adoption and Fostering
Skyline House
Union Street
London SE1 0LX
Tel. 0171 593 2000

Parent to Parent Information
on Adoption Services
Lower Boddington
Near Daventry
Northamptonshire
NN11 6YB
Tel. 01327 260 295

Post-Adoption Centre
5 Torriano Mews
Torriano Avenue
London NW5 2RZ
Tel. 0171 284 0555

Use this book for teaching literacy

This book can help you in the literacy hour in the following ways:

✓ Children can discuss the themes and link them to their own
  experiences of adoption.

✓ They can discuss the case studies and speculate about how they might
  behave in each situation.

✓ They can compare this book with fictional stories about adoption to
  show how similar information can be presented in different ways.

✓ They can try rewriting some of the situations described in the form
  of a story.

Index

Numbers in **bold** refer to pictures as well as text.